THE JOURNEY CONTINUES VOL 7

IN THE BEGINNING THEORY OR FACT HMMM??

WILLIAM HATFIELD

ACKNOWLEDGEMENTS

We are all on a journey through life! I want to thank all my family and friends who stand besides me and encourage me when times are tough.

I especially want to thank my aunt Viola for all her work in editing and preparing the manuscript of my first book for publishing. The knowledge she shared will help me to continue writing. Her confidence in me ignited a gift I never realized I had. God created me with many gifts and one of them is to be a writer. Thank you Jesus for your great love.

DEDICATION

I dedicate this book to the thirsty and hungry saints of God that desire an intimacy with the Holy Spirit like no other. My prayer is that you can find this journey as a source of encouragement, strength and power to overcome life's struggles and walk in a greater sense of freedom and relationship with the Holy Spirit and all within your sphere of influence.

PROLOGUE

Everybody is interested in the future. Questions are asked and internalized, meditated on and depending on the outcome of the meditation, reaction results. Our reactions are either fear based or faith based depending on the subject meditated on. I Have always been interested in the past especially creation. I hope you enjoy my exploration into this subject.

CONTENTS

1 PROPHETS

Prophets are an interesting group of people, especially from my perspective. I was amazed when somebody claiming to be a prophet or have prophetic abilities would show up in church for a meeting or in my personal life. Generally when prophets came to church you can feel comforted thinking the pastor has already familiar with this persons ministry and won't allow someone in who is self-serving and looking to manipulate the saints for their own agendas.

One of the things I observed in my 52 years of Christianity is that you cannot set prophets into a mold. If you attempt to do this you can and probably will lose out on a needed ministry in the church. A prophet is part of the fivefold ministry with the pastor of your local church. Ephesians 4: [11] So Christ himself gave the apostles, the prophets, the evangelists, the pastors and teachers, [12] to equip his people for works of service, so that the body of Christ may be built up [13] until we all reach unity in the faith and in the knowledge of the Son of God and become mature, attaining to the whole measure of the fullness of Christ.

[14] Then we will no longer be infants, tossed back and forth by the waves, and blown here and there by every wind of teaching and by the cunning and craftiness of people in their deceitful scheming. [15] Instead, speaking the truth in love, we will grow to become in every respect the mature body of him who is the head, that is, Christ. [16] From him the whole body, joined and held together by every supporting ligament, grows and builds itself up in love, as each part does its work.

Each of the fivefold minister as well as the saints is wonderfully and fearfully made and carries an anointing on their lives unique to the personalities God created in them at the new birth.

Another thing that impressed me was a prophet could look backwards in time and bring to light things and situations unknown to man. This of course is under the anointing of the Holy Spirit and not guesses work. The manifestations of the Holy Spirit as mentioned in

1 Corinthians 12:4-11 [4]There are different kinds of

gifts, but the same Spirit distributes them. [5]There are different kinds of service, but the same LORD. [6]There are different kinds of working, but in all of them and in everyone it is the same God at work. [7]Now to each one the manifestation of the Spirit is given for the common good. [8]To one there is given through the Spirit a message of wisdom, to another a message of knowledge by means of the same Spirit, [9]to another faith by the same Spirit, to another gifts of healing by that one Spirit, [10]to another miraculous powers, to another prophecy, to another distinguishing between spirits, to another speaking in different kinds of tongues, and to still another the interpretation of tongues. [11]All these are the work of one and the same Spirit, and he distributes them to each one, just as he determines.

The only manifestation of the Holy Spirit not in the Old Testament was tongues and interpretation of tongues. This set's this ministry apart from the Old Testament prophets. Prophet's in the old and New Testament share a lot of the same characteristics. They are human and can make mistakes. In the Old Testament mistakes were solved by stoning so get it right or die. There was not a long lineup for this ministry saying I want to be, I want to be; simply because the price was too high. In the day of grace we judge the fivefold ministry by the fruit of the spirit. Galatians 5:[19] the acts of the flesh are obvious: sexual immorality, impurity and debauchery; [20] idolatry and witchcraft; hatred, discord, jealousy, fits of rage, selfish ambition, dissensions, factions [21] and envy; drunkenness, orgies, and the like. I warn you, as I did before, that those who live like this will not inherit the kingdom of God.

[22] But the fruit of the Spirit is love, joy, peace, forbearance, kindness, goodness, faithfulness, [23] gentleness and self-control. Against such things there is no law. [24] Those who belong to Christ Jesus have crucified the flesh with its passions and desires. [25] Since we live by the Spirit, let us keep in step with the Spirit. [26] Let us not become conceited, provoking and envying each other.

I guess I am rambling because in this generation it's too easy to become known as a fivefold minister without even being called by Jesus Christ to serve his body not rule over them. Anyways let's continue this adventure. I want to look at a few Old Testament prophets that were speaking of events happening before they were even born on planet earth and had no knowledge of such events outside of God revealing it to them for our blessing and understanding. Let's start with the man who wrote the first five books of the bible. Moses wrote of events and people that existed before he was alive on the earth. Let's start at the beginning. The Beginning

[1]In the beginning God created the heavens and the earth. [2] Now the earth was formless and empty, darkness was over the surface of the deep, and the Spirit of God was hovering over the waters.

[3] And God said, "Let there be light," and there was light. [4] God saw that the light was good, and he separated the light from the darkness. [5] God called the light "day," and the darkness he called "night." And there was evening, and there was morning—the first day.

This subject may get boring as I love to research words to find the meaning because I think the meaning between Hebrew and Chaldean which the Old Testament was wrote in to our modern day English gets lost or mixed up in the translation.

2 THE BEGINNING

As I was doing research on Genesis 1:1 I found a lot of root words that causes curiosity. I decided not to add all of them because there is just too much to digest in one sitting.

The Beginning

1 In the beginning God created the heavens and the earth. **2** Now the earth was formless and empty, darkness was over the surface of the deep, and the Spirit of God was hovering over the waters.

The word beginning is an interesting word

◀ 7225. reshith ▶

Word Origin
from rosh
Definition
beginning, chief
NASB Translation
beginning (19), choice (2), choicest (3), finest (2), first (16), first fruits (7), foremost (2).
The word that sticks out to me in all the Hebrew meanings of the word beginning is FIRSTFRUITS.
To me it suggests that the beginning wasn't the

start and conclusion of the matter. It suggests that God has something in mind. The law of first fruits says that when the first part is holy then the remainder is also holy. This provides a mechanism for us to move things out of the worldly system into the Kingdom of God where different rules apply. So if the beginning being the first fruits is holy unto God then eternity which is the main part is holy as well unto God.

The word created is interesting…

#1254 ברא bara' {baw-raw'}

a primitive root; TWOT - 278; v

—Hebrew Word Study (Transliteration-Pronunciation Etymology & Grammar)

1) to create, shape, form

  1a) (Qal) to shape, fashion, create (always with God as subject)

    1a1) of heaven and earth

    1a2) of individual man

1a3) of new conditions and circumstances

1a4) of transformations

1b) (Niphal) to be created

1b1) of heaven and earth

1b2) of birth

1b3) of something new

1b4) of miracles

1c) (Piel)

1c1) to cut down

1c2) to cut out

2) to be fat

2a) (Hiphil) to make yourselves fat

- **#1254a**.
- בָּרָא
- **bara** (135b); a prim. root; *to shape, create*:—
- **NASB** - brings about(1), clear(2), create(6), created(32), creates(1), creating(3), Creator(4), cut them down(1), make(2), produced(1).

- **#1254b**.

- בָּרָא
- **bara** (135d); a prim. root; *to be fat*:—
- **NASB** - making yourselves fat(1).

We have two words that describe creation ayth (owth)

This word suggests miracle appearing totally completed at origin bara' {baw-raw'}

This word according to scholars mean intact and perfect

With these two meaning we could read Genesis **1:1** in the first fruits God completed the heavens and the earth intact and perfect.

God had a plan when he created the earth. Traditional Christianity says the earth and man is only six thousand years old. True science says the earth may be as old as one hundred and fifty million years old. This could account for the evidence of dinosaurs found by archeologists.

My personal opinion is mankind is only six thousand or so years old, but the earth is older than man. I have never been a young earth creation believer. I have always leaned towards an old earth ideology. Now if Genesis 1:1 says complete, intact and perfect, what is the word was in Genisis1:2 doing there?

3 WHY IS WAS

[2] Now the earth was formless and empty, darkness was over the surface of the deep, and the Spirit of God was hovering over the waters.

Pronounce: **haw-yaw**

Strong: H1961

Orig: a primitive root (compare 1933); to exist, i.e. **be or become**, come to pass (always emphatic, and not a mere copula or auxiliary):-- beacon, X altogether, be(-come), accomplished, committed, like), break, **cause, come (to pass)**, do, faint, fall, + follow, happen, X have, last, pertain, quit (one-)self, require, X use. H1933

The word haw-yaw suggests something happened to the earth to cause it to or come to pass being formless and void. God never created a formless and void mess then started putting it together like a puzzle. The verse should read [2] Now the earth **became** formless and empty, darkness was over the surface of the deep, and the Spirit of God was hovering over the waters.

What happened for it to become formless and empty with darkness over the surface of the deep? I think 2 peter might begin to shed some light on this. 2 Peter 3:5-6 King James Version (KJV)

[5] For this they willingly are ignorant of, that by the word of God the heavens were of old, and the earth standing out of the water and in the water:

[6] Whereby the world that then was, being overflowed with water, perished:

This verse is not talking about Noah's flood. Suggest a flood at creation genesis ch2 suggests recreation. Okay let's put something together. Genesis1:1 God created the heavens and earth completely intact and perfect, then Genesis 1:2 become a mess. What Happened and when?

Traditional Christianity says everything happened the same day. Through my study of the word meditation and prayer I have to lean to the pre gap theory. Which says there is a time gap between Genesis 1:1 and Genesis 1:2? How long of a gap do you think? A thousand years, a hundred thousand or maybe into the millions? I don't know and Cn only speculate with every bible scholar who has endeavored to research this topic.

What happened? Well my opinion is during the gap time the fall of Lucifer happened. I believe the fall of Lucifer caused judgment which messed up the whole universe. I believe there is evidence of this in scripture.

4 THE FALL OF LUCIFER

In Job 38**God Challenges Job**

1Then the LORD answered Job out of the whirlwind, and said,

2Who *is* this that darkeneth counsel by words without knowledge?

3Gird up now thy loins like a man; for I will demand of thee, and answer thou me.

4Where wast thou when I laid the foundations of the earth? declare, if thou hast understanding.

5Who hath laid the measures thereof, if thou knowest? or who hath stretched the line upon it?

6Whereupon are the foundations thereof fastened? or who laid the corner stone thereof;

7When the morning stars sang together, and all the sons of God shouted for joy?

The sons of God here are bene Elohim

which is translated angels in other scriptures.

Who Are The Bene Elohim?

Bene Elohim – also known as ben Elohim, bene Elohim, bene elim or b'ne Elohim. Their name means "Sons Of God". And they are an order of angels and archangels. They are also a subdivision of the choir of angels known as Thrones. Although, sometimes they are even equated to the **Thrones**.

Angels rejoiced at the creation of the heavens and the earth. Among those angels was an angel named Satan which was not his original name, Satan means adversary. Lucifer was his original name which means a light bearer. I believe the fall of Lucifer happened in the dateless past somewhere in between Genesis 1:1 and Genesis 1:2. That fall set the universe into an entire chaotic state.

In Isaiah **4** That thou shalt take up this proverb against the king of Babylon, and say,

How hath the oppressor ceased! the golden city ceased!

5 The LORD hath broken the staff of the wicked, *and* the sceptre of the rulers.

6 He who smote the people in wrath with a continual stroke, he that ruled the nations in anger, is persecuted, *and* none hindereth.

7 The whole earth is at rest, *and* is quiet: they break forth into singing.

8 Yea, the fir trees rejoice at thee, *and* the cedars of Lebanon, *saying,* Since thou art laid down, no feller is come up against us.

9 Hell from beneath is moved for thee to meet *thee* at thy coming: it stirreth up the dead for thee, *even* all the chief ones of the earth; it hath raised up from their thrones all the kings of the nations.

10 All they shall speak and say unto thee, Art thou also become weak as we? art thou become like unto us?

11 Thy pomp is brought down to the grave, *and* the noise of thy viols: the worm is spread under thee, and the worms cover thee.

12 How art thou fallen from heaven, O Lucifer, son of the morning! *how* art thou cut down to the ground, which didst weaken the nations!

13 For thou hast said in thine heart, I will ascend into heaven, I will exalt my throne above the stars of God: I will sit also upon the mount of the congregation, in the sides of the north:

14 I will ascend above the heights of the clouds; I will be like the most High.

15 Yet thou shalt be brought down to hell, to the sides of the pit.

16 They that see thee shall narrowly look upon thee, *and* consider thee, *saying, Is* this the man that made the earth to tremble, that did shake kingdoms;

17 *That* made the world as a wilderness, and destroyed the cities thereof; *that* opened not the house of his prisoners?

18 All the kings of the nations, *even* all of them, lie in glory, everyone in his own house.

19 But thou art cast out of thy grave like an abominable branch, *and as* the raiment Lof those that are slain, thrust through with a sword, that go down to the stones of the pit; as a carcase trodden under feet.

20 Thou shalt not be joined with them in burial, because thou hast destroyed thy land, *and* slain thy people: the seed of evildoers shall never be renowned.

21 Prepare slaughter for his children for the iniquity of their fathers; that they do not rise, nor possess the land, nor fill the face of the world with cities.

22 For I will rise up against them, saith the LORD of hosts, and cut off from Babylon the name, and remnant, and son, and nephew, saith the LORD.

23 I will also make it a possession for the bittern, and pools of water: and I will sweep it with the besom of destruction, saith the LORD of hosts.

24 The LORD of hosts hath sworn, saying, Surely as I have thought, so shall it come to pass; and as I have purposed, *so* shall it stand:

This is not a judgment over an actual king of the earth but over Lucifer. Look at verse 13 and

14. I will ascend into heaven, I thought he was always in heaven. Exalt his throne above the stars of God, interesting. He has a throne suggests he is a ruler of some kind. Above the stars of God says he is below what we understand is space. Ascend above the heights of the clouds to the sides of the north. Putting it together I think Lucifer was a ruler on the earth and ruled over somebody. He was leading worship on the mount of congregation and wanted to ascend to a higher place. Lucifer before the fall wanted to exalt his throne and be like the most high God. Let's look at another passage of scripture. Ezekiel 28: **1** The word of the LORD came again unto me, saying,

2 Son of man, say unto the prince of Tyrus, Thus saith the Lord GOD; Because thine heart *is* lifted up, and thou hast said, I *am* a God, I sit *in* the seat of God, in the midst of the seas; yet thou *art* a man, and not God, though thou set thine heart as the heart of God:

3 Behold, thou *art* wiser than Daniel; there is no secret that they can hide from thee:

4 With thy wisdom and with thine understanding thou hast gotten thee riches, and hast gotten gold and silver into thy treasures:

5 By thy great wisdom *and* by thy traffick hast thou increased thy riches, and thine heart is lifted up because of thy riches:

6 Therefore thus saith the Lord GOD; Because thou hast set thine heart as the heart of God;

7 Behold, therefore I will bring strangers upon thee, the terrible of the nations: and they shall draw their swords against the beauty of thy wisdom, and they shall defile thy brightness.

8 They shall bring thee down to the pit, and thou shalt die the deaths of *them that are* slain in the midst of the seas.

9 Wilt thou yet say before him that slayeth thee, I *am* God? but thou *shalt be* a man, and no God, in the hand of him that slayeth thee.

10 Thou shalt die the deaths of the uncircumcised by the hand of strangers: for I have spoken *it*, saith the Lord GOD.

11 Moreover the word of the LORD came unto me, saying,

12 Son of man, take up a lamentation upon the king of Tyrus, and say unto him, Thus saith the Lord GOD; Thou sealest up the sum, full of wisdom, and perfect in beauty.

13 Thou hast been in Eden the garden of God; every precious stone *was* thy covering, the sardius, topaz, and the diamond, the beryl, the onyx, and the jasper, the sapphire, the emerald, and the carbuncle, and gold: the workmanship of thy tabrets and of thy pipes was prepared in thee in the day that thou wast created.

14 Thou *art* the anointed cherub that covereth; and I have set thee *so*: thou wast upon the holy mountain of God; thou hast walked up and down in the midst of the stones of fire.

15 Thou *wast* perfect in thy ways from the day that thou wast created, till iniquity was found in thee.

16 By the multitude of thy merchandise they have filled the midst of thee with violence, and thou hast sinned: therefore I will cast thee as profane out of the mountain of God: and I will destroy thee, O covering cherub, from the midst of the stones of fire.

17 Thine heart was lifted up because of thy beauty, thou hast corrupted thy wisdom by reason of thy brightness: I will cast thee to the ground, I will lay thee before kings, that they may behold thee.

18 Thou hast defiled thy sanctuaries by the multitude of thine iniquities, by the iniquity of thy traffick; therefore will I bring forth a fire from the midst of thee, it shall devour thee, and I will bring thee to ashes upon the earth in the sight of all them that behold thee.

19 All they that know thee among the people shall be astonished at thee: thou shalt be a terror, and never *shalt* thou *be* any more.

Notice verse 13 been in Eden the garden of God and walked up and down in the midst of the stones of fire. This was not the garden of Eden on the earth but the garden of God in paradise. 2 Corinthians 12:4 Paul was caught up to paradise. From the text we see Lucifer as an anointed cherub that covers and tabrets and pipes were built into him. Most bible scholars don't understand thou hast walked up and down in the midst of the stones of fire. Throne in Isaiah 4 doesn't literally mean a chair to sit in but is an idiom for authority.

So trying to put this all together we get Lucifer has a place of authority under heaven and leads angels not men into God's presence in worship. Now here is a theory that makes sense to me trying to put this all together. THE DATES BIBLE GIVES THIS IDEA God created the earth and had a pre Adamic race inhabiting it. Angels possibly because in the book of revelation where the dragon causes a third to fall, they may be the angels he had authority over. I think Jeremiah 4 speaks of a judgment.

[22] "My people are fools;
    they do not know me.
They are senseless children;
    they have no understanding.
They are skilled in doing evil;
    they know not how to do good."

23 I looked at the earth,
  and it was formless and empty;
and at the heavens,
  and their light was gone.
24 I looked at the mountains,
  and they were quaking;
  all the hills were swaying.
25 I looked, and there were no people;
  every bird in the sky had flown away.
26 I looked, and the fruitful land was a desert;
  all its towns lay in ruins
  before the LORD, before his fierce anger.

27 This is what the LORD says:

"The whole land will be ruined,
  though I will not destroy it completely.
28 Therefore the earth will mourn
  and the heavens above grow dark,
because I have spoken and will not relent,
  I have decided and will not turn back."

Verse 25 says there were no people. Couldn't be Noah's flood because there were eight people in the ark. Theory only but I think this section of scripture is Jeremiah prophesying backwards of a pre Adamic race. our future talks about a thousand year reign of Jesus and eventually God the Father making his home with mankind on a new earth. Genesis 1:2 flows with Jeremiah 4:23.

Theory suggests the fall of Lucifer caused a condition for God to destroy all of the pre Adamic world, people and cities to the point where archeologists would never be able to dig them up again and recreate everything again in six days. God flooded the earth so that the remains of the pre Adamic race is so encrusted under the oceans that you can't dig them up again and probably start some kinds of new religion. Here is a thought God told Adam to replenish the earth. If there wasn't some kind of human on the earth before wouldn't God say populate the earth rather than replenish the earth?

I don't know of a pre Adamic race outside of the angels who have been here a long time. I can't find any scientific evidence that we are mankind 2.0. Jeremiah 4 is rather interesting scripture that could fit in the gap. This is what I am sure of, genesis 1:1 God created the heavens and earth completely intact and perfect. I believe He spoke this natural universe into existence. He spoke and bang it came into existence miraculously suddenly complete and perfect without sin and death. I believe that there is a time gap between genesis 1:1 and 1:2. I believe that during that gap is when the fall of Lucifer happened and it caused extreme judgment causing a recreation of the six days model. There are so many creation theories out there that if I listed all of them we would have more questions than answers. I lean to the gap theory and the fall of Lucifer during that time frame. My research into this subject in no ways takes from the work of Jesus at the cross. My curiosity of an anointed cherub caused my study to take place.

Another thing I noticed about Lucifer was his covering of precious stones. I want to take a closer look at this because Lucifer has nine of the twelve that were on the chest plate of the high priest. He also has nine of the twelve foundations of the New Jerusalem.

5 THE STONES OF LUCIFER

When a study is made of the archangel the anointed cherub Lucifer, it is apparent that this being was initially garbed as a priest of the heavenly temple of God. He was robed similarly to the Jewish High Priest. There was one exception. The Jewish High Priest had a breast plate of 12 gems while Lucifer's breastplate was made with just 9 gems. He is missing the third row. Lucifer's stones from Ezekiel 28, you were the model of perfection, full of wisdom and perfect beauty. You were in Eden the garden of God, every precious stone ordained you: **ruby, topaz, and emerald, chrysolite, onyx, and jasper, sapphire, turquoise, and beryl.** Your settings and mountings were made of gold; on the day you were created they were prepared. You were anointed as a guardian cherub, for so I ordained you. You were on the holy mount of God. You walked among the fiery stones. You were blameless in your ways from the day you were created.

All the jewels on the High Priest robe from Exodus 28:16 foursquare it shall be being doubled; a span shall be the length thereof, and a span shall be the breadth thereof. 17: And thou shalt set in it settings of stones, even four rows of stones: the first row shall be a **Sardis, a topaz, and a carbuncle**: this shall be the first row. 18: and the second row shall be an **emerald, a sapphire, and a diamond**. 19: and the third row **a ligure, an agate, and an amethyst**. 20: and the fourth row a **beryl, and an onyx, and a jasper**: they shall be set in gold in their inclosing's. 21: and the stones shall be with the names of the children of Israel, twelve, according to their names, like the engravings of a signet; every one with his name shall they be according to their twelve tribes.

The New Jerusalem, the Bride of the Lamb

[9] One of the seven angels who had the seven bowls full of the seven last plagues came and said to me, "Come, I will show you the bride, the wife of the Lamb." [10] And he carried me away in the Spirit to a mountain great and high, and showed

me the Holy City, Jerusalem, coming down out of heaven from God. [11] It shone with the glory of God, and its brilliance was like that of a very precious jewel, like jasper, clear as crystal. [12] It had a great, high wall with twelve gates and with twelve angels at the gates. On the gates were written the names of the twelve tribes of Israel. [13] There were three gates on the east, three on the north, three on the south and three on the west. [14] The wall of the city had twelve foundations, and on them were the names of the twelve apostles of the Lamb. [5] The angel who talked with me had a measuring rod of gold to measure the city, its gates and its walls. [16] The city was laid out like a square, as long as it was wide. He measured the city with the rod and found it to be 12,000 stadia in length, and as wide and high as it is long. [17] The angel measured the wall using human measurement, and it was 144 cubits thick. [18] The wall was made of jasper, and the city of pure gold, as pure as glass. [19] The foundations of the city walls were decorated with every kind of precious stone. The first foundation was jasper, the second sapphire, the third agate, the fourth emerald, [20] the fifth onyx, the sixth ruby, the seventh chrysolite, the eighth beryl, the ninth topaz, the tenth turquoise, the eleventh jacinth, and the twelfth amethyst. [21] The twelve gates were twelve pearls, each gate made of a single pearl. The great street of the city was of gold, as pure as transparent glass.

Stones present in all three situations;

Lucifer	High Priest	New Jerusalem
: Ruby	Sardis	ruby
Topaz	topaz	topaz
Emerald	Emerald	Emerald
Chrysolite	carbuncle	chrysolite
Onyx	onyx	onyx
Jasper	Jasper	Jasper
Sapphire	sapphire	sapphire
Turquoise	agate	turquoise
Beryl	beryl	beryl
	Diamond	diamond
	Ligure	jacinth
	Amethyst	Amethyst

Some of the names of the gemstones have changed over the years but notice Lucifer is missing three of the twelve. Maybe it has something to do with his fall?

6 **LUCIFER'S LIMITATIONS**

Lucifer even before his fall is limited as he is a created being. Ezekiel 28: **14** Thou *art* the anointed cherub that covereth; and I have set thee *so*: thou wast upon the holy mountain of God; thou hast walked up and down in the midst of the stones of fire.

15 Thou *wast* perfect in thy ways from the **day that thou wast created**, till iniquity was found in thee. I believe it I safe to say God taught Lucifer everything he knows. Not everything God knows, but everything Lucifer knows.

The word covereth in verse 14 is a symbolic word for guardian angel. So when you look at the stones Lucifer had compared to the high priest and the New Jerusalem you may ask, is there a connection?

Perchance when God was designing the natural world and mankind, He put Lucifer in charge of watching over the nation of Israel. With the connection of stones with Lucifer and the

New Jerusalem I wonder if God didn't put Lucifer in charge of building that massive city.

All through the scriptures we see God the Father who has a desire to live with His creation mankind. You can see this in the feast of tabernacles, God dwelling with man.

When I look at verse 14 thou art the anointed cherub, I wonder is that an anointing built into you at creation, or is it something else? God created Lucifer as the highest angel in God's angelic kingdom. Lucifer was the anointed cherub (Ezekiel 28:14; Isaiah 14:12, 13). Lucifer's Reign as the anointed cherub that **covereth was God's most high priest in the mountain of God** (Isaiah 14:12-14; Ezekiel 28:13-17).

A high priest represents man before God and a prophet represents God to man. In my thinking based on 1 John 2:20, 27 [20] But you have an anointing from the Holy One, and you know all things. [27] But the anointing which you have received from Him abides in you, and you do not need that anyone teach you; but as the same anointing teaches you concerning all things, and is true, and is not a lie, and just as it has taught you, you will abide in Him. When you have an anointing to do something it continually motivates you to fulfill that anointing. In the beginning you may not be good at it but by reason of use you become mature discerning between good and bad.

I am going to throw a speculation out to you on how things played out. God created Lucifer for a JOB TO FULFILL. God gave him the job of building the New Jerusalem and with each floor finished Lucifer was given a gem stone symbolic of each floor completed. With each foundation completed he received a gemstone and became closer to walking in his destiny as the anointed cherub that covers. Lucifer was also the worship leader with musical instruments built into him. Besides sounding great he was starting to look pretty awesome with each gemstone given him as a reward for a job well done building the great city.

Just after completing the ninth floor Lucifer asks God, "why am I building this huge city?" God informs him of his plan to make a creation called man in his own image and likeness. Lucifer asks, "Do I get to rule over them?" thinking to himself , I am the greatest and a piece of cake as well. To Lucifer's surprise God responded "NO" "you will serve them by watching over them, protecting them and show them how to worship." Lucifer was enraged because God was going to create a race of beings after all the 5 I will's Lucifer desired in his heart. Lucifer decided to overthrow God and lost. Ezekiel 28: **16** by the multitude of thy merchandise they have filled the midst of thee with violence, and thou hast sinned: therefore I will cast thee as profane out of the mountain of God: and I will destroy thee, O covering cherub, from the midst of the stones of fire.

17 Thine heart was lifted up because of thy beauty, thou hast corrupted thy wisdom by reason of thy brightness: I will cast thee to the ground, I will lay thee before kings, that they may behold thee.

Judgment came Lucifer was cast down to the earth that was and judgment came destroyed everything leaving the earth without form and void as mentioned in Genesis 1:2. Lucifer became Satan the adversary. Satan seeks to steal kill and destroy. Can you see some of the attributes of Lucifer's job in heaven turned evil because of pride and hatred? The music of the world is about drugs, sex, murder, violence, suicide and most of the lusts of the flesh. The nation's under the influence of Satan blame Israel for so many things they are innocent of. Satan wants to destroy the very nation he was supposed to watch over as Lucifer.

7 ADAM WAS CREATED TO BE EVERYTHING LUCEFR'S I WILL DECLARED

"The 5 'I Wills' of LUCIFER"

Let us consider the five "I WILLS" of Lucifer as found in Isaiah 14:1314:

1) "I WILL ASCEND INTO HEAVEN." Lucifer wanted to mount up or scale to the heavens. He desired to occupy the highest heavens: to probe, and to penetrate the kingdom of the infinite God. He wanted to have a very HIGH position!

2) "I WILL EXALT MY THRONE ABOVE THE STARS OF GOD." Lucifer's position and service before God's throne was not enough. He wanted a throne from which he could exercise final authority and make decisions pertaining to the angelic host ("the stars of God"). He wanted to rule over all the angels. God had made him an exalted angel, but Lucifer wanted to be exalted even more. (He was not content to shine as the

"morning star"; he wanted to shine as the star of stars--with a brilliance that would far outshine all the other stars (even as the sun's brightness makes all the other stars fade away so that you cannot even see them during daylight hours).

3) "I WILL SIT ALSO UPON THE MOUNT OF THE CONGREGATION." He desired to sit or be enthroned in the highest place having all the angelic assemblies in submission to him. He wanted to be the center of attention. He wanted to be IDOLIZED by all.

4) "I WILL ASCEND ABOVE THE HEIGHTS OF THE CLOUDS." "Clouds" are often used in the Bible to speak of the glory of God (see Matthew 24:30; Acts 1:9; Rev. 1:7). Lucifer coveted God's glory for his own. He failed to acknowledge that his glory and beauty all came from and was dependent upon God. In his sinful pride, Lucifer wanted a glory that would impress and dazzle all creatures.

5) "I WILL BE LIKE THE MOST HIGH." He wanted to be EQUAL with God and to take God's place as Possessor and Ruler of all. He wanted to become

a completely independent creature, responsible to no one.

Let's take a look at the scripture to see the creation of man. Genesis 1: [26] Then God said, "Let Us make man in Our image, according to Our likeness; let them have dominion over the fish of the sea, over the birds of the air, and over the cattle, over all the earth and over every creeping thing that creeps on the earth." [27] So God created man in His *own* image; in the image of God He created him; male and female He created them. [28] Then God blessed them, and God said to them, "Be fruitful and multiply; fill the earth and subdue it; have dominion over the fish of the sea, over the birds of the air, and over every living thing that moves on the earth."

5) I will be like the most high….. Let Us make man in Our image, according to Our likeness;

2) "I WILL EXALT MY THRONE ABOVE THE STARS OF GOD….; let them have dominion over the fish of the sea, over the birds of the air, and over the cattle, over all the earth and over every creeping thing that creeps on the earth. Ephesians 2:6 Good **News Translation**
In our union with Christ Jesus he raised us up

with him to rule with him in the heavenly world. Ephesians 2:6 covers I will 1,2,3,4.

Psalm 8:5 **English Revised Version**
For thou hast made him but little lower than God, and crownest him with glory and honour.

God's original intention was to make man a little lower than himself but still in His class. Our image and likeness suggests same class of being.
Psalm 82:6 English Revised Version
I said, Ye are gods, and all of you sons of the Most High.

John 10:34 English Revised Version
Jesus answered them, Is it not written in your law, I said, Ye are gods?

1 John 3: [9] Whoever has been born of God does not sin, for His seed remains in him; and he cannot sin, because he has been born of God.

1 Corinthians 6:3 English Standard Version
Do you not know that we are to judge angels? How much more, then, matters pertaining to this life!

These Attributes are the very attributes Lucifer desired to have. You want to see people freak out personalize psalm 82:6 and speak it aloud.

8 IN CONCLUSION

I am not trying to create a new teaching or doctrine but merely exploring one of the many creation theories out there. I shared my idea about the gap theory that I wrote on in this book to a pastor and right away he said I should be careful because curiosity killed the cat, and told me that he preaches his theory because he preaches literally and doesn't try to make the bible say what it doesn't say. My response on curiosity killed the cat was and satisfaction brought him back.

We both agreed this topic was very controversial and the only way we are going to know is when we get to heaven and go to the massive library there and look it up.

Is it beyond your imagination that God wanted his best angel to watch over His creation man? Hebrews 1:14 King James Version (KJV)

[14] Are they not all ministering spirits, sent forth to minister for them who shall be heirs of salvation?

Hebrews 1:14 New International Version (NIV)

[14] Are not all angels ministering spirits sent to serve those who will inherit salvation?

Father God has an exciting destiny for each of us that go far beyond our imagination.

This book is about my continued journey through my Christian life and with the many versions of the bible available today I decided to fulfill Acts 17:11 **New International Version** Now the Berean Jews were of more noble character than those in Thessalonica, for they received the message with great eagerness and examined the Scriptures every day to see if what Paul said was true.

I love doing word studies because it brings the scripture to life more than traditional Christianity presents.

I was curious about Lucifer because I never heard a pastor of any church I associated with preach on the subject. I have read the bible from cover to cover many times and my favorite version is the New King James version. One thing I noticed over and over again was gemstones in the high priest garments. Gemstones adorning Lucifer and the gemstones in the foundations of the New Jerusalem. They were all the same stones but Lucifer was missing three of the twelve.

Again I am not trying to be controversial but am trying to be a good Berean and study the scriptures. My goal is to have the best journey of my Christian life and grow in my knowledge of God's word and understanding of His ways.

EPILOGUE

We are all at a different place in our spiritual growth and relationship with the Holy Spirit. I chose to share this adventure of my life hoping it will encourage you to go after the Holy Spirit and grow in your relationship with Him. I don't see myself as anybody great or extraordinary. I am just a regular person with a heart for God. I have committed myself to him to be whatever he wants me to be and go where ever He wants me to go. It's been an adventure and a journey

ABOUT THE AUTHOR

52

BIO

William carries the anointing of a prophet and psalmist. He is also a Bible teacher, author and international speaker. He operates in all of the Spiritual gifts. He uses the gifts as the Holy Spirit wills. One of William's great desires is to lead others to Christ and to follow Holy Spirit wherever He leads.

YOU CAN VISIT MY WEBSITE
WWW.PSALMISTWILLIAM.CA
FOR ENCOURAGING PSALMS AND TO BUY OTHER BOOKS I HAVE WRITTEN

www.ingramcontent.com/pod-product-compliance
Lightning Source LLC
Chambersburg PA
CBHW032131050726
47590CB00008B/3047